The Book of Thieves

The Book of Thieves

Stephanie C. Fox, J.D.

QueenBeeBooks

Bloomfield, Connecticut, U.S.A.

Library of Congress Cataloging-in-Publication Data
Name: Fox, Stephanie C., author.
Title: The Book of Thieves / Stephanie C. Fox.
Description: Connecticut: QueenBeeBooks, [2011].
Identifiers: ISBN 978-0-9996395-5-9 (paperback)
Subjects: BUSINESS & ECONOMICS / Banks & Banking. TRUE CRIME / General. LAW / Government / Federal.

www.queenbeeedit.com

Cover design by Stephanie C. Fox
Cover art by Stephanie C. Fox
Printed in the United States of America

Also by Stephanie C. Fox

The Bear Guarding the Beehive

Nae-Née
Birth Control: Infallible, with
Nanites and Convenience for All

Vaccine: The Cull
Nae-Née Wasn't Enough

New World Order Underwater
The Nae-Née Inventors Strike Back

What the Small Gray Visitor Said

Intrigue On a Longship Cruise

Elephant's Kitchen
– An Aspergirl's Study in Difference

Almost a Meal –
A True Tale of Horror

Scheherazade Cat:
The Story of a War Hero

An American Woman in Kuwait

Hawai'i – Stolen Paradise:
A Travelogue

Hawai'i – Stolen Paradise:
A Brief History

This story is dedicated to
the next generation of citizens
in the hope that they will
take their country back,
and keep it.

I wish that the
previous generations
had thought ahead more
on their behalf.

Table of Contents

The Tale of the Thieves

I will tell you the story of how a great country lost its security.

There once was a great country with people, leaders…and thieves.

The people did not notice the thieves, and the leaders did not see that the thieves were thieves, because the thieves were called by other names.

The thieves had labels that made them seem benign and respectable, such as bankers, brokers, investors, corporate attorneys, and other such titles. The thieves handled money, and most of it belonged not to them, but to the people.

The thieves knew that it wasn't their own money, but they did their best to control as much of it as they could, and to keep as much of it as they could for as long as they could. The thieves also worked hard to find ways to take money away from people and to never, ever give it back to them. After all, that is what makes them thieves.

The people did not notice what was happening until it was too late, because they had a great system of laws that applied to the thieves and to themselves. They thought that this would be enough. But it wasn't enough, because laws need honest people to make sure that they are followed and not eroded with lots of little conflicting rules and regulations.

No system sits on its own, taking care of itself, no matter how well written it is.

It took a while for the people to realize this.

Meanwhile, the thieves had a wonderful time.

The name of the country is Oblivion, and its people are the Oblivious.

The characters in this tale are: The Banksters, the Dealers, the Trustee, the Key Holder, the Obliterated, the Observers, the

Assembly, the High Court Judges, and the Chief.

Together, their actions and inactions, their crimes and carelessness, ruined Oblivion.

None of this is new; it has happened to other nations in the past, and will happen again.

It happens because some people are greedy criminals, and others don't pay attention.

This is an alarming tale, perhaps too frightening for children. Then again, perhaps not…

It is a cautionary tale, and cautionary tales are exactly what children should be told.

The Land of Oblivion

The Land of Oblivion was a huge, beautiful country. It stretched across an entire continent, and had many different climates, landscapes, species of plants and animals, and fish. It had mountains and plains, forests and deserts, lakes, ponds, rivers, streams, and waterfalls.

Many of these beautiful places were set aside, not to be built upon, and called parks. The people of Oblivion went to the parks when they wanted to see and hear and smell nature, and to enjoy the quiet, away from the ambient light of buildings, streets, and connecting highways.

The country had cities and towns, sectioned off into smaller parts of the whole of Oblivion, whose local governments sent representatives to the beautiful Marble City, where the national government of Oblivion was located.

Each city and town of Oblivion was an interesting place, with a history of its own. There were monuments, historic houses, and athletic fields for the people, as well as small businesses and large ones, where people could go to buy books or eat ice cream, restaurants of all kinds, and clothing stores.

In between the cities and towns were farms that grew fruits, vegetables, and livestock. When the farmers weren't too busy, they invited people to come and pick fruit and then buy it. They also taught children about farming by giving tours of their property and operations.

Oblivion had many universities and museums and libraries for its people to enjoy, so a large portion of the population was quite well educated. The nation's elected officials and business leaders had attended these schools, as had its authors, scientists, artists and musicians.

The museums showed people all sorts of fun and fascinating things: machines that took people into outer space and back, ancient art, not-so-ancient art, everyday objects from various points throughout time, items from other cultures in other countries, and innovations in science.

Every part of Oblivion had a museum about the Founding Forebears, who were the people who had begun the nation by declaring its independence and writing its laws. The best of these were in the beautiful Marble City, which also had monuments to each Founder.

The Marble City had huge, beautiful palaces in it that were devoted to carrying out the laws of the Founders, and to making more laws that were based on the original laws. The purpose of this was to serve and to protect the people of Oblivion, and their money.

This was very important work, because without money, even the best legal system fails.

The Loophole

The people of Oblivion thought they had a great legal system, and were very proud of it.

The system was over two centuries old, and the Founding Forbears had done an excellent, careful, well-thought-out job of setting it up. There were checks and balances on three branches of political power, which were held by the Chief, the Assembly, and the Courts. It was the Chief, the Assembly Members, and the Judges of the High Court who worked to preserve and protect the laws in the beautiful palaces of the Marble City.

The Chief was expected to represent the interests of the country as a whole and its people after being elected to a term of four years, and he or she could only be elected twice. The duties of the Chief included meeting and visiting with foreign leaders, signing or not signing new laws presented by the Assembly, and appointing judges to the High Court.

The Book of Thieves

The Assembly, a group of people who had been elected from all over Oblivion, was responsible for writing new laws and passing them. These potential laws were called bills.

This meant that each potential law had to be discussed and voted upon.

A bill was not a law until it was signed by the Chief.

Making laws was a very complicated endeavor.

The reason for this was that the Assembly was made up of two Sections, a Mansion and a Palace, and both had to approve a bill before it could be presented to the Chief for signature. This led to a lot of discussion, delays, and arguments, because the members of both Sections were elected from two different Factions.

These Factions were called the Grabbers and the Altruists.

The Book of Thieves

Each Faction had logical arguments for its opinions about how the government should manage the country and its assets, and each Faction had not-so-logical arguments as well. This was why it could take such a long time to present a new law.

The Chief was elected from either the Grabber or the Altruist Faction also, and this meant that unless most of the Assembly was from the same Faction, the Chief could not get much done. Naturally, the Chief had things that she or he wanted to accomplish during the term, just as the members of the Assembly did.

If a bill came to the Chief that the Chief disagreed with, the Chief would not sign it. At that point, it would go back to the Assembly for revisions. This often meant that bill never became law. The people all learned about this in school and felt happy with the system.

But there was something that most of them did not know about it.

This little-known fact was not a secret; it was simply a detail that most people didn't take the trouble to notice and memorize. However, it was of critical importance.

If the Assembly wrote and passed a bill, there was one more step before the Chief saw it.

This step was called the Conference Table.

The Conference Table was a group of senior Assembly people who had the power to make small but significant changes to a bill before presenting it to the Chief. The difference that this made could, and often did, have the effect of making a bill say the complete opposite of what its original writers had intended.

The changes were always written in such a way as to require a very careful reading and rereading before this became clear, and the bills tended to be rushed through the political process so that this would not be noticed.

The Book of Thieves

The Chief might or might not notice that the bill up for signature had changed.

If he or she noticed and objected, the Chief could refuse to sign it into law.

It seemed strange at first to anyone who learned about the Conference Table that the Chief might ever sign such a bill into law even knowing that it now said the opposite of what it had said when it was first written.

But if the person was told about the Pressure Pointers, the situation made sense.

However, it should be stated that making sense is not at all the same as making right.

This was not right. It simply was the way that things functioned in Oblivion.

The Pressure Pointers were people who were paid huge sums of money by businesses who could lose money – or just make less money – if a particular bill became law. So they paid people who had been sent to law and business schools to pressure the Chief and the members of the Assembly not to pass any such law.

Sometimes this didn't work, but often it did.

It worked because the Chief and the Assembly members needed much larger sums of money in order to get elected and re-elected to office, and the Pressure Groups had the money and were happy to give it to them.

This was the flaw in the system, which was called a Loophole.

Individual people did not have enough money to fight it.

Perhaps that was why those who knew about it turned their attention away from it.

There was that, and the fact that there were other ways to fight for fair laws.

Once in a great while, the people would gather together and fight in those other ways, such as with lawsuits in the Courts, or with petitions to the Assembly members who then worried that the people would not vote for them again, but that didn't happen often enough.

It fell to the Courts – and often the High Court at the top of the court system – to balance things out. The judges on the High Court were chosen by the Chief and approved by the Assembly, and once seated, they remained until they chose to leave.

The High Court was the place to take a complaint about a major point of law that affected the entire country of Oblivion. Decisions from the High Court became law that was as binding as bills that were signed by the Chief or passed by the Assembly.

Each High Court Judge was a human being with a law degree and either academic or professional experience…or both…with her or his own personal opinions. No one could avoid having their own opinions. It was just part of being human and living. This meant that each Judge agreed more with either the Grabbers or the Altruists.

The Book of Thieves

The people felt happy and secure about this part of Oblivion's system too. It meant that neither faction could have its way all of the time to the exclusion of the other one.

But the High Court was very busy with many cases, so most of the laws in Oblivion came from the Assembly and the Chief, complete with the Loophole. And that wasn't the whole story.

The checks and balances part of Oblivion's system of government was that a bill passed into law could negate a decision of the High Court, or a decision of the High Court could cancel out a law passed by the Chief and the Assembly. This kept the Loophole in place.

The Pressure Pointers and the big, wealthy businesses benefitted from the Loophole. So did many of Oblivion's wealthiest people. The businesses included Oblivion's largest banks, its largest and most successful stores and other resource vendors, shippers, and insurers. Many of them belonged to the Grabbers Faction.

The Book of Thieves

The Altruists tended to be individual people who did not earn huge sums of money, plus academics with advanced degrees, small business owners, teachers, and occasionally some wealthy people who thought that grabbing more than one needed to survive was wrong.

There were many other people who were either Grabbers or Altruists who were neither very wealthy nor very poor. Their incomes and educational levels varied as much as their other characteristics did. Political affiliation did not always correspond to income, as there were other issues that mattered to the people of Oblivion than money. But those are other stories.

Regardless, even without an obvious reason for the decision, each voting citizen of Oblivion was either a Grabber or an Altruist, because each person needed to say which Faction they belonged to in order to vote in preliminary elections, so each one made a choice.

The Book of Thieves

There were many banks, large and small, to manage the assets of the country, which came in many forms: land, crops grown by farmers, buildings, bridges, highways, natural resources, and taxes from the people's earnings. The bankers would keep the money that resulted from trading in these assets and the people's earnings in neatly labeled accounts.

Each one of the people had one vote – each woman and each man, no matter who they loved or married, no matter what they looked like, and no matter how much money or property they possessed or managed to earn.

Oblivion had schools and hospitals, roads, bridges, ferries, airplanes, outer space transports, museums, libraries, movie theaters, symphony halls, sports arenas and fields, ice rinks, famous monuments, national parks, zoos, and plenty of homes.

The maintenance on these things was paid for through taxes on the people's property and earnings, and also with the profits generated when banks held money.

The Book of Thieves

The people of Oblivion considered this whenever they had an opportunity to vote, and registered their opinions with Assembly Members by calling them or sending letters to them.

That was why the money had to be guarded by bankers who would not violate the trust that the people felt towards them when they handed their money over to be held, watched, and eventually given back to them.

At the top of this system of bankers was a man whom the Chief appointed to track the money of Oblivion, to manage how much was out in use by the people at any one time, how much profit could be generated from bank holdings, and to oversee rules for the banks and bankers of the country. He had to be someone who understood money and who could be trusted.

This man was, not surprisingly, called a Trustee.

We shall look at him shortly.

The Tools of Thievery

The Thieves had several tools at their disposal for taking in money.

Oddly, taking in money wasn't the act of thievery; it was their intent to keep it forever.

The agreement that the thieves made when they took it in was to keep it for a while and to keep it safe, and to have it ready to give back to the people of Oblivion if and when they either needed it or wanted it.

Until then, the thieves were allowed to possess it, to benefit from it as long as they didn't take unnecessary or large risks with it, and to profit from it within those limits.

The problem – the theft – was that the thieves decided those limits were too…limited.

That was not their decision to make.

But about the tools…

The tools included bank accounts, pension funds, mortgage payments on housing loans, insurance payments, and fees from transactions at the National Casino.

A bank account was a fairly straightforward means of acquiring control of someone else's money. People came to the bank to find a safe place for their money, which the bank provided. But because allowing the bank to hold onto the money was a matter of personal choice, and because there were many banks to choose from, the banks had to offer something more. The thing that they offered was interest payments. The longer the person left the money with the bank, the more interest built up in the account. Also, the more money in the account, the more interest accrued, and sometimes at a higher percentage rate.

A pension fund was money that a citizen's employer took out of the citizen's paycheck each week (or pay period – they varied with employers) and which the employer deposited in an account controlled by the government. When the citizen retired, the government would give it back, in small amounts over time. This fund was managed by the Trustee, who was appointed by the Chief, and whose duty it was to protect the fund just as a private banker was expected to do.

Mortgage payments were installments that citizens paid back to banks at regular intervals – months, typically – on loans for houses and condominiums. To qualify for a loan, a potential borrower had to show the bank that he or she had a significant portion of the price of the home to put down up front. Next, the borrower had to have a job or business that was producing a regular income in order to prove that he or she could meet the mortgage payments. The payments usually lasted for three decades. If the borrower lost the job or business and was unable to continue making the payments, the bank could then possess the house, and the borrower would lose the down payment, the past mortgage payments, and be out on the street.

An insurance payment was something that was made to protect a citizen against risk. Life is full of risk: illness, injury, and loss of property due to severe weather, accidents, other damage, or theft. The people of Oblivion would buy insurance policies to protect themselves from having to bear the entire cost of such unfortunate events. In return, they felt a bit safer from financial loss than they would without such policies. What the insurer got out of the deal was the use of the policy holders' money, with the understanding that the insurer, just like a banker, must be ready at any time to pay out lump sums if an unfortunate event did in fact occur. This meant that the insurer, just like a banker, had a duty not to take any great risks with the money.

Finally, there were fees that could be collected from transactions at the National Casino. The sources of these fees were trades at the National Casino by big corporations and private citizens of Oblivion, and ultimately, the pay that Oblivious people chose to use for such things.

Eighty years earlier, laws had been made to regulate banks and the National Casino.

Those laws were now being whittled away at by the Pressure Pointers.

No laws had been made to regulate the insurers.

The Trustee

The land of Oblivion needed someone to oversee all of the people and entities in its realm that generated or handled money. There were laws that applied to this, plus other rules called regulations. Some of these regulations were extremely complex – seemingly endless in their numbers, details and cross-references – so a human being was needed to manage it all.

The Chief was responsible for finding someone to do this, to be the national banker.

The Trustee was expected to have an education and work history that prepared him or her to handle money and regulate big businesses.

The Trustee was also expected to be emotionally disinterested in the rewards reaped by big businesses, always putting the interests of the people of the land of Oblivion first.

The Book of Thieves

Honesty was a quality that the people needed above all else in the Trustee, because if big businesses were put first, the people would lose their money.

The people kept their money in individual bank accounts – both savings and checking – retirement accounts built up over a lifetime of work, small allotments of shares in the National Casino, and various other forms that were tied to the workings of big businesses.

If big businesses were allowed to serve themselves without regulations, the people's money would not be safe.

If the people lost their money, they would not be able to get it back.

They needed an honest Trustee to protect it.

The Chief chose a man whose credentials were impeccable.

The man he chose wore glasses that looked like huge magnifying lenses and was going bald. He was a thin man, not very tall but not short either, who spoke well and read what everyone who attended the parties read. He wore nice suits and ties and walked smoothly among the people he met wherever he went. He certainly seemed like the sort of person who could and would inspire confidence.

The Chief did not know it, but being liked was very, very important to this man. It was so important to him that he would do whatever his friends wanted him to do, no matter what it was, as long as it meant that he would still have a good time at the next parties.

The man had gone to a very old and respected school, called the Ivy League University. It got this name because the lovely old buildings of its campus were covered with ivy in warm weather. The school was also famous, as old as the land of Oblivion, and staffed by the best and most famous professors.

The man had joined the Insider Club there, and majored in economics.

Economics is the study of money, finance, and business.

The man had even done some graduate work there, which meant that he had spent some extra time studying after earning his basic degree. He spent three years in graduate school at that university, and met many people at parties there. Students attended them not just for fun, but to make influential friends who could help them when they left school and went to work.

The man took full advantage of these parties, and met people who were experts in the field of economics, but economics was a very quiet, serious field. The majority of the people who studied it were not popular, not cool, and the not life of the parties. He wanted to be the life of the parties – all parties, all of his life.

Many of the best, most enjoyable parties, were given by the Insider Club, a secretive organization for the protégées of Thieves. Thrilled to have been admitted to its inner sanctum, the man attended any party given by the Insider Club. Its parties were opportunities to meet and interact with future as well as present leaders in many fields, not just economics.

The Chief did not know how much the man valued these connections and friendships.

Neither did the Assembly Members, who had to meet him and talk to him before approving him as Trustee of the National Reserve of the Land of Oblivion. All that they saw was his work record, which looked great, so they approved him.

The man was very happy. Being Trustee would make him very popular at parties.

The Trustee made up his mind to stay in his wonderful, exalted new position for as long as he possibly could. To do this, he intended to make sure that each Chief after the one who appointed him would like him just enough to want him to stay on.

The Trustee's job was not an elected office, and it didn't have term limits, so he anticipated no problems with this plan. One of the Trustee's duties was to come to the Assembly regularly to answer questions about the Thieves. But he didn't come very often, and when he did appear, he only took one or two questions, claiming that he didn't have time for any more. The Assembly had not passed laws to require that the Trustee appear more often and that he stay and take all of their questions.

The Trustee found that all of the people he met – both at work and at parties – were politicians and Banksters. He didn't meet any of the regular people of the land of Oblivion.

That made forgetting their interests easy for the Trustee, and he stayed for forty years.

The National Casino

For those of the Oblivious who liked to gamble with their livelihoods, an institution existed that was known as the National Casino.

The National Casino was housed in a beautiful white marble palace on an island that was almost completely built up into a city. It was located on the southern end of the Island, and often, when the weather was nice, a huge flag of the land of Oblivion stretched across its façade.

The city had five sections, and the Island was just one of them. There was another, smaller island that made up another section, plus part of the mainland for another section, and finally a much larger, longer island that stretched perpendicular to the island district had the remaining two sections on it.

The Island was named for an ancient tribe of people who had lived there before other people found it and decided to join them on it. One of the museums, which was not far from the National Casino, contained art and artifacts from this Tribe, and exhibits illustrating that story. They were the founders of Oblivion, and they were the original Thieves of it as well, because they had tricked the Tribe into accepting almost nothing for the Island.

The part of the city that was on the Island was the most desirable of the districts. It was a pleasant place with parks, lovely apartments and condominiums, gourmet grocery stores, bakeries and restaurants that featured the cuisines of cultures from all over the planet, historic sites, museums, a zoo, monuments, an opera house, a ballet troupe, a huge theater district, and many famous comedians and performers of all kinds.

In short, the city was a fun place, even a bit luxurious for nearly all of its residents, though it was rapidly becoming more and more expensive to live on the Island. But the Island was the most convenient and most enjoyable of the five sections of the city, so the people who owned its buildings constantly worked at finding excuses to raise the prices for residential ones.

The Book of Thieves

The people who sought residences on the Island either had more money than most of the Oblivious, or else they struggled to afford a place as prices rose but their incomes did not. They made the effort to afford homes on the Island because they needed to be near work, and because the Island was such an enticing playground.

The Island was the ideal location for the National Casino.

One reason for this was that the government, with the Chief, the Assembly, and the High Court, were all hours south of it, in another beautiful city. The other reason was that the Island was just so nice to live on.

Regardless, the National Casino was a place that was in news reports all day, every day.

The National Casino was very different inside from the shining white palace that it presented on its outside. Inside, it was mostly just one huge, cavernous room. The floor of the room was hard and cold, made of granite. The ceiling was high – several stories high. Most of the light was provided by electrical devices, and most of the electrical devices, whether or not their function was solely to provide illumination, emitted a lot of light.

The room was called the Trading Floor.

What was traded on the Trading Floor was a long list of things, each of which was given its own short set of initials on the electrical devices. This was what the reports flashed updates of all day long. The reports were not about the people who worked in the National Casino, though there were many of them.

The employees who worked inside the National Casino wore blue jackets and stood at small computerized stations all day, looking at readouts in front of them and then up above at huge electronic boards with yet more readouts, making odd, urgent gestures. They bought or sold shares of businesses, which were called Securities, and in things called Necessities, which included corn, wheat, cocoa, coffee, and fossil fuels. They did this on behalf of banking and investment firms, insurers, and individual citizens of Oblivion.

Employees of the Banksters, whom we shall read about shortly, also sent representatives to the National Casino. These employees were called Dealers, and they were not seen on the Trading Floor. They met with the supervisors of the blue jacketed workers, who were called Pit Bosses, who took care of their transactions.

All the while, the symbols and initials of the Securities and Necessities streaked across the electronic boards at the National Casino, and on news channels on television stations and on a display in the theater district of the Island. The point of this was to provide constant updates of the financial values of each Security and Necessity.

The reason for all of these updates was they changed over and over again throughout each workday. Nothing was constant, and without inside knowledge of each business, predicting the values was nearly impossible. Having that knowledge was what made the difference between making a profit at the National Casino and losing all of one's money.

Only a few people had inside knowledge of many businesses at once, and they worked hard to keep it that way.

These were the Banksters, groups of bankers and insurers who controlled the largest, oldest, most secretive, and wealthiest banks and insurance companies.

The Banksters

The Banksters in Oblivion were men in beautiful suits and ties who controlled most of the nation's money. Their job was to maintain something called liquidity – the continual flow of money – for banks, businesses, and individual citizens. Another name for the Banksters might be risk-takers, because they knowingly assumed the risk of losing money in order to make it. This was their choice, however, so they should not be pitied if they lost any.

To accomplish this, they kept money tied up in many ways, including bank accounts – which was not strange, since the Banksters business was banking, insurance, and trades of shares at the National Casino.

The goal of the Banksters was to grab as much money as they could while giving little or nothing in return, either to the government of Oblivion, or to any of the Oblivious people who kept their money in accounts managed by the Banksters. This was obvious during the winter holidays, when the Banksters always awarded themselves huge bonuses on top of their pay.

The Banksters had attended the most exalted colleges, universities, and professional schools in the land of Oblivion. No one knew them as Banksters, however. They called themselves bankers, and were men in suits who ran huge businesses. They dressed like most citizens of Oblivion when in their formal clothing, except that their clothes were very expensive.

The Banksters were a complicated lot to keep track of, many groups with many names. There were the Golden Bags, who were the oldest, largest and most aggressive of all. Next, there were the Tribe Chasers, named for the city on an island where the National Casino was located. All of the Banksters kept their main offices on that island, and close to the National Casino.

After Golden Bags and Tribe Chasers, there were several other, smaller Banksters, each with names that were well-known throughout Oblivion. Unfortunately, the people of Oblivion didn't know or bother to find out much else about them. The other Banksters' names were Layout Sibilants, Oblivious International Gang, Bare Stricter, and Fuhrer Securities. That last one was a foreign investment bank, but it was well-situated to play with the others.

The Banksters lent out money to Oblivious businesses and citizens, and even to a foreign government, which led a nation called Sphinx. That nation was directly to the east of Oblivion, across the huge ocean, and inland. Sphinx was the nation that had formed a wonderful democracy thousands of years ago, one that was the first of its kind.

Fortunately, the people told themselves, there were many, many laws and regulations in place to rein in the greed of the Banksters. Even better, the Assembly made more regulations all of the time. Added to this was the Trustee, whose expert judgment oversaw the regulations and could be counted upon to police the Banksters. Thus reassured, the people of Oblivion sat back and trusted the Trustee to handle the Banksters, and occupied themselves with other things, unconcerned about their money and security.

The Codification

Several decades ago – eight, to be specific – it was decided that a new law was necessary in order to protect the people of Oblivion from the greed of Banksters. This was because the Banksters had managed to acquire most of the nation's wealth. They had achieved this thanks to a lack of regulations on the size of their individual businesses, which had grown too big, which had reduced both their numbers and the amount of competition that they faced, and thanks to a lack of regulations on their business practices, which had resulted in mass unemployment.

The Banksters were having a wonderful time because they could take more and more for less and less, and they grew fat and smug, feeling entitled to all that they had amassed.

The Chief at that time, an unusual man who was wealthy yet a member of the Altruist Faction, decided to act when the land of Oblivion was suffering from the effects of rampant poverty, which had been caused by Thievery. Thievery comes in cycles, and the cycle that Oblivion was suffering from was particularly vicious. This was the first time that Oblivion had experienced such intense suffering, which was called the Great Depression.

That Chief had written the new law. It regulated the actions and size of the Banksters.

The Assembly Members who worked with that Chief had agreed with the law that he wrote and had passed it. The Judges of the High Court at that time had also seen fit, when those laws came before them for review, to affirm them.

The checks and balances had backed each other up.

The people of Oblivion were thrilled; the new law looked fair because the law and its rules and forms were short, simple, and to the point. They were greatly relieved to see a way out of the Depression.

The Book of Thieves

But the Banksters who ran the biggest banks and insurance groups at that time were unhappy with the new transparent, simple system. They loved to control most of the nation's wealth and did not care about the suffering of others. If the rest of the Oblivious citizens had no money and no jobs, it must be their own fault, they said.

Those Banksters were very sorry to find that suddenly stealing from the funds that the Banksters managed had become difficult and in many instances nearly impossible, so they began to look for ways to get around the new law.

The Assembly was expected to write new rules and regulations as it saw fit, as was the Chief. Every few years, new Assembly Members and a new Chief were elected, so the new office holders would be looking for votes, and to look for votes, they would need campaign money. The Banksters still had plenty of that, even after taxes, because they paid lawyers and accountants to find regulations that granted exceptions to their tax obligations. They also paid

The Book of Thieves

Pressure Pointers to visit Assembly Members.

This gave the Banksters some ideas for getting around the new law.

One way was to make more rules and regulations exist, rules and regulations that would grant exceptions to the law, and others that would seem to require special actions on the part of the Banksters while actually granting them permission to access more money that didn't belong to them while giving almost none of it back.

To do this, the Banksters hired teams of Pressure Pointers to visit and harangue and even threaten the members of the Assembly. The Pressure Pointers moved to the city where the government institutions were so that they could do this all day, every day. This was expensive, but it enabled them to steal so much more money that they didn't mind.

It worked; the Assembly proceeded to enact laws that functioned as extensions of the original law. These laws were in fact called rules and regulations, and they were as binding as the original one. Time passed, and soon there were so many of them that they became a book.

The Banksters also hired expensive lawyers to fight cases on their groups' behalf in the Courts, and paid extra to plead final appeals in the High Court for more lenient rules, which also became part of the book.

Because each law had a code with which to identify it and thus list it in order – both by date of enactment and by category – the book was known as the Codification.

Law schools and accounting schools devoted entire courses to it, because lawyers and accountants specialized in interpreting it. They profited from careers spent aiding and abetting the theft that the Codification enabled, and the Banksters were happy to pay them for it. It was a lot cheaper than accepting and obeying the original law.

As the years and decades went by, the book only grew bigger and more confusing, snarling related codes together as they were cross-listed and voided and resurrected and added to like a psychotic seizure. So did the forms that citizens, bankers, insurers and others had to fill out each year. It seemed normal to the Assembly Members, who made a living in politics.

The people of Oblivion accepted the Codification, focusing on other things as soon as they could look away from their own tax forms, bank loans, mortgages, and insurance payments. They even believed that the more codes that were added to the Codification, the fairer the system would be. Expenses would be shared in equal percentages by all, thought the people, if they just played by these rules.

The assumption that the Thieves would play by the rules was wrong, but the people didn't notice what was happening, because they couldn't make sense of the Codification.

The Thieves were happy.

The Codification worked perfectly.

The Key Holder

The Key Holder was a smart, well-educated woman who worked under the supervision of the Trustee. She had chin-length hair that was slightly wavy, wore pearl earrings and a matching pearl necklace, and nice skirt-suits with high-heeled shoes. Her clothes weren't as expensive as those of the Banksters – that would have been unseemly for a government official – but they were very nice, silk blouses and suits nonetheless.

Like the Trustee, the Key Holder had been educated at the finest schools in the land of Oblivion. She had done her undergraduate work at Ivy League University, and then gone on to the State University of Obfuscation, because it had an excellent reputation for preparing people to work in finance. She had even, unlike the Trustee, stayed long enough to earn her Ph.D. in economics. Like the Trustee, she had joined the Insider Club, and knew the Banksters.

The Book of Thieves

She was a smooth talker, very skilled at interacting with everyone she met, and the Chief had been very impressed with her when he was reviewing candidates for the post of Key Holder. After asking the Trustee about her and hearing high praise, the Chief approved of her appointment.

The Trustee was very happy to have someone like her working with him, tracking every change in the value of Oblivion's monetary unit, the Lollard. She was very good at her job, which was to log his every decision about the National Reserve and field requests from the Banksters, who had secured seats for themselves on the National Reserve Board. The Board informed the Trustee and the Key Holder about the finances of the nation's banks.

The Key Holder listened sympathetically to whatever the Banksters said or asked.

One request that came into her office was for an exception to an important rule.

The Book of Thieves

The rule – a crucial one found in the original Necessities Law, before the first Codification was issued – was for the Banksters to be treated differently from the producers and marketers of Necessities.

Producers of Necessities such as cocoa and corn took a risk when they grew these things. The weather might be bad, or a flood could wash all of their work and materials away, leaving them with nothing.

Users of Necessities took a risk too. They needed to be able to count on goods actually being available to buy, regardless of weather and floods. When such things happen to Producers, there are fewer goods to buy. That, when unregulated, can cause prices to go up.

The goal was to have something in the market and at a good price. The law provided that the Producers and Users could count on a fair market price every time they brought their goods to market – not too high, not too low, but just right so that everyone could stay in business.

But there was one more player that kept this system running: the Gambler.

The Gambler's role was to assume a risk by buying up lots of Necessities from Producers whenever they were available and holding them until a User came along to buy them. How long that could take was unknown, but at least the Gambler provided a place to keep the Necessities. The Producers and Users met the Gambler at this in-between point, and the market continued to function. The risk to the Gambler was one that was knowingly assumed.

The Gambler risked periods of time with no earnings when Necessities were not moving through the market. Also, the Gambler had to work within limits because the Necessities Law would not allow the Gambler to buy up all of anything, a practice that was called hoarding. The reason behind this was to prevent the Gambler from gaining an unfair advantage and manipulating the market price.

If that happened, the market price couldn't possibly be fair.

Under the original law, the Gamblers – who were the Banksters – risked low profits.

For several decades, the Banksters worked with this restriction, but they didn't like it.

To the Banksters, a decent profit was an amount that far exceeded what the other participants in the market made, and one that was raked in at almost no risk. This was in exact opposition to the Necessities Law and they knew it.

Finally, when the Key Holder who knew them from the Insider Club was appointed, they saw their chance. One by one, they went to see her, being careful not to put their requests into writing. They each described the difficulty that the Necessities Law presented for them, moaning piteously that it prevented them from making a decent profit. They framed their request in such innocent, sorrowful terms that their old friend listened with concern, forgetting about the risk that the Producers and Users had to face.

The Book of Thieves

The Banksters were taking a risk just as the Producers and Users were, they complained.

She nodded her head as she read their requests, and agreed.

With that, she wrote the first of thirteen letters granting an exemption to the rule.

Soon the Banksters had acquired and hoarded all of the cocoa, all of the corn, all of the wheat, and so on. They raised the market price of each Necessity and insisted that it was fair.

The Producers soon found that farming was more expensive than profitable for many of them, and that they could not earn a living that way anymore. They sold their farms off to Banksters who then combined them and ran huge businesses with huge machines and few citizens working on the new, huge farms. The market prices of Necessities continued to rise.

The Users had to pay these prices in order to produce chocolate, bread, cereal and other products that the citizens needed on a daily basis. This made their business costs rise so that the smaller ones failed and the larger ones – also owned and run by Banksters – grew larger.

This went on and on, even though the citizens were puzzled as to how the cost of these goods had gone up so much over such a short time. Many of them passed the time telling younger ones what they used to pay for such things.

The same thing happened with the oil that Oblivion needed to fuel its cars and houses.

It took two decades for the market price to falsely inflate to such an extent that the citizens became truly unhappy, but they didn't see what they could do to stop it. They didn't see it because the Gangster managed to keep the thirteen exemption letters hidden, and to restrain themselves from ever mentioning them.

Once the Thieves controlled most of the Necessities, fewer and fewer citizens had jobs with which to pay for them. The Thieves knew that it was only a matter of time before they would not be able to keep taking huge, falsely inflated amounts of money for themselves, that at some point soon, the bubble would pop and the music would stop, but they didn't care.

They could just walk away from the situation and enjoy the money at that point.

Until then, the party continued for them, while the Oblivious people didn't notice.

They were very grateful indeed to the Key Holder.

The Dealers

The Banksters were a few people who worked at the very top levels of their groups. Their plan to take money for little in return required the assistance of other people. There were plenty of willing individuals in the banks to help them do it.

In addition to the honest workers in the banks, there were Dealers.

Dealers knew everything that bankers did – they just didn't care about the customers.

All they cared about was making money and running away with it.

This meant that they could only grab small amounts of money when compared with what the Banksters were able to get control of. That was because they had to give the Banksters a large cut of whatever they took in, and because once the deed was done, the Dealers had to disappear quickly before the shocked and angry citizens who realized that they had been used found them and reported them to the lawyers who worked for the government.

Dealers did this through mortgages, breaking faith with borrowers, by investing the loans in worthless, mislabeled Securities, and by selling them to individual citizens who wanted to try their luck at the National Casino.

They gave home loans to people who could not possibly have afforded to buy any home at all. Too many people got these loans, which falsely inflated home values, like a bubble waiting to burst. When that happened, the Banksters turned the people out onto the streets with their credit ruined, so that they could not even get apartments. They became homeless.

When the Dealers were finished, the banks that they worked for were heavily in debt and had lost the money that they were expected to hold at low risk. They had allowed high-risks deals, and now something had to be done.

The Book of Thieves

The director of Golden Bags, the largest one of all, a nasty little man with a phony expression on his face, demanded that the government get his bank all of the money that it was owed immediately. This would mean raiding pension funds, but he didn't care.

He was pulling a bluff. He knew that if he didn't do this first, the fraud would either be exposed and Golden Bags would fail, or else some other Gangster would do it, get the money, and grow to a size that threatened Golden Bags. After that, Golden Bags could still fail.

This nasty little man also knew that Oblivious International and the others could have made a deal with Golden Bags, but that wouldn't have been as profitable for him.

With that, the large ones swallowed up the smaller ones, breaking a one hundred and twenty-year-old law against allowing any business to grow so large as to crowd out competition. It was the Dealers who had aided and abetted in this crime, but they were nowhere to be found.

The Obliterated

The Obliterated were the individual citizens of Oblivion.

They occasionally attempted to earn money by participating in transactions at the National Casino. This meant using a Dealer in order to buy or sell a Security or a Necessity, or multiple shares of them.

It also meant that the Obliterated could live anywhere in the land of Oblivion and still do this, because they could just call their Dealer and he or she would handle the whole thing. The way it worked was, a Player, acting on only the information that was available to the general public via television, Internet, or newspapers, would call his or her Dealer and instruct him or her to buy or sell a particular number of shares of something.

The Dealer would then do so, with no responsibility for the outcome.

If the Player's purchase went up in value, that was great.

If the Player's purchase lost all value, it didn't matter to the Dealer.

Either way, the Dealer got a small fee and the National Casino made money.

Most of these investment attempts were disastrous to the Obliterated.

The Banksters just raked in the money from the Obliterated.

Many of the Obliterated lost their life's savings this way.

Some went crazy and killed themselves. Some killed others before killing themselves.

Whenever the citizens of Oblivion heard about a Player's suicide, they would nod their heads and say that it was foolish to try to make a profit at the National Casino, that only the Banksters had any actual hope of doing that, and that the killer shouldn't have tried at all.

The Book of Thieves

If only he had had the sense to just do something less risky, he would still be alive, they said. After all, they added, the Player who failed should have known better than to try to make money through the National Casino, because everyone knew that only the big boys – the Banksters – could do that.

Because it was so risky to try to make money at the National Casino, most citizens just relied on jobs and small businesses to make money. It just seemed safer and saner. Only the big businesses, the groups run by the Banksters, had enough information available from talking to one another in person to make money this way. For them, there was almost no risk.

That was why most citizens just quietly worked at their jobs and applied for mortgages – special bank loans – in order to buy homes to live in. Most homes in Oblivion were houses that had to be bought. Only in big cities could people expect to find a larger number of residences that were for rent than for sale. The vast majority of Oblivious people did not live in cities, so they had to buy their homes.

Buying a home was difficult, however.

The reason for this was the cost: it cost almost a lifetime's worth of pay to buy a home.

Because people needed to use some of their money along the way for other important things such as food, clothing, and transportation, they could only spend a portion of their earnings on a home. The only way to afford a home, therefore, was to go to a bank and borrow the money after saving enough for a down payment, and to show that she or he was working. The citizen would then slowly pay the money back with interest payments, which were the profits that the banks earned for letting people use that money.

At least, that was how things were supposed to work, and according to the regulations.

Instead, the Dealers committed fraud by not requiring any money down and by offering low interest rates that would rise dramatically in a few years. This was called a balloon mortgage, because of the sharp, abrupt, and steep rise that would then occur. When that happened, the payments would be too high to make.

Many of the people who signed up for these loans did not realize that this was happening because the Dealers talked so fast, and because they were so friendly before the papers were signed. Balloon mortgages were enticing to people who did not make enough money to buy homes under the regulations. Once they signed the contracts, the Dealers were gone.

This was because the Dealer had sold the mortgage to another bank far away, for a fee. That bank had then done the same thing, and so on and on, with each one trying to get rid of the loan before the balloon rose. The Dealers made millions of Lollards this way.

The unfortunate Obliterated, who had acted in good faith while relying on individuals who were experts in their fields to honestly guide them through these deals, were in a panic. They tried to get help, but there were so many of them that the government found it difficult to find the time to listen to them. Special courts were set up to hurry the cases along.

The paperwork – the legal documents – of the loans looked okay at first glance, which was all that a citizen with no lawyer could expect from a judge, and many of them couldn't afford one. This was sad because a closer look at the papers would have shown the fraud: the dates of each step of the loans did not make any logical sense. They showed that the loans had been received after they were sold to the next Dealer.

Without a lawyer – usually a volunteer, a nice one who worked for no pay – the person who had signed a balloon loan swiftly lost the case, became homeless, and was unable to recover the money that she or he had lost.

It was very upsetting to see that the banks sent lawyers with stacks of files on the balloon work of the Dealers, files that were full of lies that took little or no effort to see…if only the judge had not been overwhelmed and in a hurry.

There were millions of houses that could not be paid for or bought by enough people to recover the money lost by the banks. The Dealers were gone with the money that they had stolen, leaving the Banksters to fight over the rest and recover by eating one another's groups up.

When that happened, many, many people who had worked diligently and honestly for the Gangster group suddenly had no jobs. Those people were Obliterated in the system too, because they had trusted it and followed the rules, only to lose everything.

Now it was too late to save the Obliterated…too late for the Obliterated who had pensions, insurance policies, loans that they couldn't pay, and no place to live. With no job, one could not hope to pay a loan, contribute to a pension, or meet any obligation.

The Book of Thieves

A vicious, endless, hopeless future of debt yawned like an abyss under the Obliterated.

The Observers

The people whose job it was to gather information and report it to others were called Observers. Nothing seemed to escape their notice. Observers traveled all over Oblivion and elsewhere to discover news, talking to people, looking at publicly available documents, attending lectures and conferences, and watching what large groups of citizens or individual ones did.

The Observers reported on things like new laws passed by the Assembly and signed by the Chief, judgments of the High Court, natural disasters, innovations in science and engineering, changes in education, historic preservation, monuments, and even famous actors. The stories that the Observers produced were either broadcast on television and radio as conversations or read to viewers, and they were written as articles that people could read in papers and over the Internet.

It was the Observers who also collected information on the National Casino.

Observers tended to specialize in the type of news that they sought, because the job was so time-consuming. It was more efficient that way. The ones who researched financial information missed a lot until it was already happening or worse yet, was over with.

Still, there were accidents, and there were convenient opportunities.

These things enabled the Observers to discover how Oblivion's financial system had collapsed. They found out about the Key Holder's thirteen secret letters. They found out about the balloon mortgages. They found out about the Securities and Necessities bubbles – how they were created, and their consequences, which were dire, and had been a long time in the making.

They found out that insurance companies, which had never been regulated, had lost the money that they had been entrusted with in the bubbles. They could not fulfill their duties to pay for health care and to rebuild homes lost to floods, fires, earthquakes, or storms. To avoid legal problems, the insurers paid Codifiers and Obfuscators to find excuses not to pay, citing parts of the citizens' insurance policies that had been deliberately written to be as confusing as possible.

Finally, the Observers learned that the governments of cities, towns, and states all over Oblivion had been tricked into signing up for balloon loans –to repair aging infrastructures – and couldn't pay the interest rates. They were selling and leasing highways, bridges, railroads, and even parking meters…to wealthy foreigners. The parking meters were particularly galling, because the foreigners charged fees every day, including holidays. By the time the leases were up, the highways and parking meters would need new loans for new work. But what was sold was gone, chipping away at the sovereignty of Oblivion. There was no way out of that.

When the Observers found all this out, they were furious.

They tried to explain it to the people of Oblivion, only to find surrender and resignation.

It only upset them more.

The Sudden Flushing Sound

A flushing sound – the one that represented Oblivion's financial security, of its sense of sovereignty in its properties, and of its hopes for future insurance on property and health care disappearing into a vast cesspool of non-redemption – only seemed sudden.

The fact was that it had been building up for decades.

But when the lever was first pushed on the toilet that was Oblivion's void of a regulatory system on mortgages, securities and necessities, properties, insurers, and conflicts of interest, it took awhile for anyone to notice.

That is because people don't like to focus on the sound of a toilet flushing.

The sound of a toilet flushing represents the departure of the most disgusting things that one would rather not even notice let alone expend the effort to forget.

So the Oblivious people didn't notice – at least, not until the deed was done along with the inherent damage – that some spoiled children had played with their most valuable possessions by standing over a toilet and flushing them, bit by bit.

Imagine a child with a beautiful pearl necklace standing over a toilet.

Or don't…we wouldn't want that flushed.

Imagine the child dangling the digital draft of a novel that could easily win a Pulitzer Prize, if only a publisher could see it.

Flushed, gone.

Imagine that child holding a collection of stem cells with the formula that would cure cancer cultured into them – plus the only copy of the data that explained how it was done – and flushing that away.

Where were the parents, you might ask?

The Book of Thieves

How could they have been so inexcusably careless as to just let it happen?

Why didn't they pay attention and prevent this?

Well, some might say, it's just a kid, and kids don't know any better.

But a bunch of Banksters, Dealers, a Key Holder, and a Trustee?!

They knew exactly what they were doing, they were not children, and they had done it anyway out of pure selfishness. They had no excuse, but acted as though they had done the most natural, reasonable things that anyone could be expected to do with other people's money.

Still the outraged people of Oblivion raged.

The responses did not help the situation.

Well, boys will be boys. At least, that was how the Trustee and Key Holder saw it. The Banksters had played with the valuables and lost them. What else could you expect of Banksters?

It was the same blasé attitude that many people had around little kids.

That attitude was, don't leave your things lying around unattended, because little kids will mess with them.

The only way to protect what matters to you from children and criminals is to guard it.

The Oblivious had not done so.

They had ignored what the Banksters and Dealers were doing, and had not demanded that the Trustee and Key Holder police them, just as people who see children running wild often do.

To say that this was extremely and suicidally foolish would be to state the obvious.

But in the land of Oblivion, the obvious tended to go unnoticed.

The Book of Thieves

Why?

The People Who
Wouldn't Pay Attention

The people who lived in the country with those thieves did not notice what was happening to their great nation until it was too late.

They did not notice that the laws that had been put in place to protect them were being eroded and chipped away at bit by bit by the thieves.

They did not notice that their land and monuments, their highways and bridges, their historic buildings and parks, were being sold little by little.

Instead, the people enjoyed themselves with a lovely menu of distractions.

The Thieves offered plenty of engaging distractions.

There were huge sporting events – several for each season.

The Book of Thieves

There were talents shows for people who liked to sing and dreamed of empty fame.

There were reality shows for those who enjoyed watching other people live lives that differed from their own, lives that they envied or simply wanted to catch brief glimpses of.

There were shows that took place in faraway tropical paradises.

But that wasn't all; the Thieves also offered other forms of entertainment.

The other entertainments often cost money, which the Thieves pocketed. After all, they had invested other people's money in those entertainments, and bought shares in the businesses that produced them, knowing with Insider Club certainty that those particular businesses would in fact make lots of money. The Thieves knew this before the Obliterated even knew that the businesses were being set up.

The Book of Thieves

There were video games by the hundreds for sale that the people could spend money on.

There were huge motor vehicles of all kinds to play with: all-terrain jeeps, armored cars to drive in peaceful areas for those who wanted to pretend that they were at war, snow mobiles, water-jets, monster trucks with wheels bigger than their cabs, and so on and on. Even better, the Thieves knew that these toys would require large quantities of a Necessity: oil.

There were shopping malls and discount stores and outlet shops for those who liked to hunt and gather new things every couple of weeks.

None of these things were absolutely necessary to survival; they were just fun.

There was yet another distraction that the thieves presented: political rivalries.

The Factions of the Grabbers and the Altruists offered distractions every election year.

The Grabbers Faction concerned itself with how much it could get for its followers.

The Grabbers told anyone who would listen that if you worked at a job you would be sure to have everything that you needed and wanted, but that if you didn't do that, you would not. This sounded logical until one considered the fact that there were not enough jobs for everyone who was willing and able to work.

The Grabbers didn't care about that angle of the story, however. Instead, they complained bitterly about taxes, saying that they should never, ever have to share any money with the people who couldn't work or who couldn't find any work.

The Altruists were just the opposite.

They thought it was perfectly reasonable to use tax money to help those who were less fortunate than themselves. They also believed in preserving the environment for the benefit of the next generation of people who would live in their country, and on the rest of the planet for that matter.

But doing so meant sacrificing some comforts and conveniences now, and consuming less. This seemed possible, however, because the Altruists could see that people all over their country were consuming more of everything – food, fuel, clothing, and other materials – than they actually needed in order to have comfortable, happy lives.

The people had an excellent way to watch all of this: Television.

There was a channel devoted to the Assembly, plus many news shows.

Unfortunately, the people gave in to distractions and only saw little bits of news.

What little they saw gave them just enough information to choose either a Grabber or an Altruist in each election, but not enough to see that things were hidden from them.

The Book of Thieves

Each person had a vote, so each person had a say in who got to hold office.

The people thought that this was a wonderful system, and quite fair.

And it was, but it had one flaw: it masked the other part of the system.

The other part of the system was the part controlled by the Thieves, who did not have to concern themselves with such inconveniences as the will of the people or term limits. Instead, they got to stay as long as they wanted to, making money with no transparency as they manipulated and thwarted the law.

The Thieves were almost invisible to the people, and so they were rarely if ever called to account for their actions in public. The people knew where the Thieves worked, but understood little about how they worked.

They could have learned about this and demanded vigilant enforcement of the old, strong laws, with no exceptions for the wealthy few, but they didn't.

They hardly thought about the good Chief who had set up the original, tight law to control the thieves. This law was called a statute – not to be confused with a statue, one of which was made to help the people remember the nice chief.

Unfortunately, the people found statues far easier to remember than statutes.

The people who had lived eighty years earlier grew up and had children, enjoying the safety that the laws gave them. Each generation had watched as Trustee after Trustee came along to oversee the Thieves using those laws, and didn't worry about the system.

Why worry?

The system had been set up so well, they thought, that there was no need to watch it.

This went on until the Trustee who enjoyed not being watched was appointed.

The Book of Thieves

By now, the people were too complacent about those laws, too confident that their interests would be represented by the Trustee, because after all, he had been appointed by a Chief that they had chosen, and reappointed by many Chiefs after that.

So the people relaxed and didn't worry about what the Trustee was doing.

After all, his very name implied that they could count on him to do the right thing.

Why worry? Why question him? Why make a fuss?

Better to trust the Trustee and enjoy life.

That was far more pleasant than to pay attention to what was happening around them.

Why didn't they pay attention?

Lots of reasons…

One was that it was easier and more fun not to.

Another was that many of them were too busy trying to earn a living to notice.

Still another was that many of them had discovered a convenient disability that prevented them from focusing their attention on any one thing for a sufficient length of time to understand what was going on around them.

This was called attention deficiency dysphasia, or ADD.

The funny thing about ADD was that some of those who had it fought the condition and went on to earn advanced degrees and had satisfying, interesting careers, while others gave in to it and lost themselves in the many distractions offered by the Thieves.

In short, the people had plenty of excuses for not paying attention, but it all came down to a matter of choice.

The Book of Thieves

The people could have paid attention and demanded full accountability from the Trustee.

The people could have demanded that laws be enacted to enable a clearer view of the Trustee's actions and that he stay and face any and all questions every month.

But they didn't.

The people forgot one of history's most important lessons, and paid the price.

The price was that the people were out of money, had too few opportunities for employment for too many people, they had lost their retirement funds, been evicted from their homes, had debts that they could not hope to repay in their own lifetime, and so they were suddenly very aware that they could not do much to help themselves, thus feeling impotent outrage and misery.

In response, the people came out into the streets near the National Casino to protest what the Thieves had done. The Thieves could see and hear the sound of the protesters, who were careful to hurt no one while keeping their message out in the open where the Observers would easily hear and see them.

The Thieves did not like the noise.

They complained to the mayor of the Island, saying that the protesters were staying on land that the Thieves owned, and that they didn't like the noise, wanted the space back, and to add insult to injury, claimed that the protesters were doing damage to the property. It was a lie, but the mayor was a wealthy man who had benefitted financially from a lack of regulation of his business, so he called the police to remove the protesters.

Hundreds of protestors were arrested, but no Thieves were arrested.

More protests were held in cities all over Oblivion with the same result.

The High Court expected to receive a request for intervention from one or both sides.

The Book of Thieves

Meanwhile, all of Oblivion watched as the nation of Sphinx began to experience the same thing. Gradually, it was revealed that the unethical business practices of Golden Bags had caused the greatest share of the misery there as well.

Still, the Thieves continued to enjoy huge profits while awarding themselves huge bonuses and salaries. One or two of them was called to answer questions at the Assembly, but they acted shocked and confused when any Assembly Member so much as suggested that they might have acted dishonestly.

The Assembly, which still failed to comprehend the fact that a lack of regulation on the Thieves' businesses had caused the misery that was crippling Oblivion's economy, did not make any new laws to address this. Instead, they wondered what was the problem, and pushed decisions farther and farther into the future so that they would only come due after the next election. Meanwhile, they talked about cutting government programs and services.

The people of Oblivion wondered how much worse the situation would have to get before they saw any improvement, or if all was lost.

Many of the nation's economists – the ones who did not have a financial stake in the outcome thanks to the pay that they drew from careers that were secure due to their credentials, experience, and forum with the Observers – told the Oblivious people that their country was now in an Economic Depression.

This was very upsetting news, because the laws that the Thieves and their Pressure Pointers had chipped away at had been made in response to a situation just like the present one. Eight decades in the past, a lack of regulation had caused this same misery in Oblivion.

Now, after a long period of ignoring the actions of the Thieves, the people of Oblivion were learning the painful lesson that the price of economic security, which had protected their ultimate sense of liberty and happiness, was vigilant attention. They had lost that.

The lesson was that the safety of a country rests with both its people and their financial security, and that those things can only be maintained by constant vigilance – constant watchfulness – and constant appreciation of this fact.

The people allowed themselves to become distracted and lost this great prize.

The price of this carelessness was terrible: lost jobs, lost land, lost savings, and with that lost control over their own country and futures.

The distractions were not worth the brief enjoyments that they had afforded.

The people abruptly understood that they could not afford distractions, but it was too late.

The Moral without Morale

I have told you these tales because I hope that if you know about what awful, terrible, inexcusably selfish things that these thieves have done, you will take care to prevent such things from happening again.

Those who don't pay attention to what is happening around them are condemned to suffer, just as those who don't study history are condemned to repeat it.

If you wish to have a sense of pride and self-respect when you think of your own people, culture and nation, you must learn these stories well and remember them.

You must never sit idly by while bad things happen.

To do so is to enable the Thieves.

It is sad to say this, but the moral of this tale is utterly without a boost in morale.

The people could only blame themselves.

So that is the moral of the story: watch, pay attention, and be involved.

The Oblivious people didn't do that, so that is why this tale offers no sense of morale.

Appendix: The Menu

We all know the land of Oblivion well. There are lots of them on this planet.

The way you can tell is by looking at their economies.

Whatever was once functional and solvent but now is not, yet has a well-respected set of laws and well-educated, civil, democratic societies with aging infrastructures is a land of Oblivious people.

Well, it seems too depressing to just leave it at that.

There isn't any sense of morale to be had when a patient is dying of acute appendicitis, unless of course a doctor can win the race to remove the infectious, diseased, unnecessary organ.

With that in mind, some possible endings to this story should be offered.

Read them all, decide which one you like best, and imagine that that is what happened in the land of Oblivion to the Oblivious after that sudden flushing sound.

And why not?

It's always nice to be able to sleep at night.

Appendix A:
The Want Ad

What can be done about the Thieves? And how do we get a trustworthy Trustee?

The second question is easier to answer than the first.

We need to look elsewhere, away from the poisonous tree of the Ivy League and the Insiders Clubs. Those places are full of only one kind of person: one who believes in privilege without responsibility, and immunity from laws, rules, regulations, and other restrictions.

We need someone who is the opposite of that.

We need someone who has never worked or even associated with the thieves.

We need someone who is not loyal to one political faction or another.

We need someone whose loyalty is the financial health and wealth of the nation.

Who better to watch and manage the thieves – and the sad reality of life is that there will always be thieves – than a trustworthy Trustee?

But getting one who is actually trustworthy is tricky.

A psychological profile should be done on all candidates, and each one ought to be shared in the interest of greater transparency. Each profile should be a matter of public record, and by law.

What would the ideal psychological profile of the ideal Trustee say?

We need someone who isn't concerned about being liked by those who are to be regulated, no matter who they are, and who will apply the laws equally and to all persons, businesses, and thieves.

This is of crucial importance because the thieves do not go out and about with the moniker "Thief" tattooed on their skin. They look just like everyone else. No criminal is going to make it easy to apply any law to any illegal activity of theirs.

To be further removed from the dangers of temptation and greed, the ideal Trustee must be independent in many ways: socially, psychologically, financially, politically, and emotionally.

We need to put out a want ad for this person, and to make this job and personality description a matter of law. We can even call this new law the Trustee Want Ad Act.

Appendix B:
The Flash Cure

Just like a flash fire or a flash cooking job, there is a simple flash cure for all this.

Burn the Codification.

It is far too complex.

This happens whenever a nation has an original law about its finances that has gotten old.

The law is made, and at first it seems like a great idea, simple, straightforward, fair and balanced on its face, and logical to apply to all.

Then time begins to pass, and thieves start to whine that they need special dispensation to ignore some of the effects of the original finance law. Every society has thieves in it.

Lawmakers listen to their complaints because the Thieves pay representatives large sums of money to pester them and worry them with the possibility of not being re-elected, forgetting that the purpose of a civil, democratic society is not to keep the same people in office forever, but to make the best and fairest laws to serve its people.

That's when codifications start.

At first they are just a few amendments to the original law, but soon they are followed by rules and regulations. Some of these regulations are well-meant, aimed at reining in the activities of the Thieves, but others are not.

The result is that gradually, a book of regulations starts to appear. Financial experts soon find that they cannot work without constantly referring to this monstrous book, which only grows larger and more complex over time...like a dreaded disease. Soon the book makes little sense and does more damage than it prevents.

But what the Oblivious fail to realize is, with a law that required trashing the Codification every decade, this wouldn't happen. Instead, the lawmakers would have to replace the entire thing with a new financial law, one law that either restated the original one or added a maximum of ten points to it – one for each year in the decade.

There would be a new Codification, one that allowed the experts to work free from worry about whatever the previous one said. But after a decade, whatever was in it would be reviewed, the best points noted for reference, and the book made null and void.

It would also have the virtue of making tax time less of a nightmare for all concerned.

Appendix C:
The Bedtime Story Ending

Fairy tale endings often feature gruesome demises for villains.

This is eminently satisfying to read, and has the desired effect of making it easy for the reader or listener to fall asleep feeling a sense of almost smug satisfaction.

So here is the happy ever after ending to The Book of Thieves:

When the people and the Chief and the Assembly and the High Court discovered the betrayal, the perfidy, and the outright breach of trust that had been displayed by the Trustee, the Key Holder, and the arrogance and thievery of the Banksters and Dealers, they were more than upset, more than furious, more than livid.

They were rabidly out for blood.

The people demanded a trial and punishment for those who they now recognized as criminals, and new laws to protect them from a recurrence of what had happened. They did this with organized protests, both in person at city parks around the nation and on the Internet.

The Chief ordered the arrest of the Trustee, the Key Holder, the Dealers, and the Banksters, and special trials of them all in the High Court, which usually only dealt with appeals and cases that could produce a new point of law. All nine of the High Court Judges were required to conduct the trials, which meant seating jurors and finding some lawyers to fight the case – one to prosecute it and one to defend.

The defendants were kept in solitary confinement so that they could not talk to one another, and given ugly clothing to wear while they were locked, which depressed them. They had only worn the most beautiful, luxurious of fabrics until now, designed by the leaders of the fashion industry, and now they had to wear flaming orange all day, every day. They also had to eat boring, cheap, bland food, another upsetting hardship after all of the power lunches, brunches, and dinners that they had eaten, each prepared by gourmet chefs.

The Observers were allowed access to the prison, which was instructed to show them the food, the clothes, the cells, and to describe the daily routines and the isolation that the once mighty Banksters had to face each day. Photographs and videos were circulated on every news channel with great enthusiasm. The people of Oblivion, awoken from their stupor, lapped it all up and discussed and described it all, happy to see that at last their political process worked.

The lawyers chosen were both famous ones. They were given full access to the secret documents of the Banksters and Dealers, and to the secret requests for immunity to the Codification and replies that had passed between the Banksters and the Key Holder and the Trustee. The lawyers had four months to study and review it all, and to prepare their cases.

A tough one who had spent her entire career fighting injustice, one who had attended the Ivy League University School of Law but had shunned the Insider Club, was the prosecutor.

An equally tough one with a long career in defending corporate interests, one who had first worked as a Pressure Pointer before going to that same law school and who had joined the Insider Club, was the defender.

Selecting the jurors proved more difficult than usual, because for once, most of the potential jurors wanted to sit on the jury rather than find some reason to be excused, but after a few weeks, twelve people had been chosen, with twelve more as alternates.

Meanwhile, the Chief ordered the Assembly to get busy drafting laws to regulate the insurers, the traders, the banks, and conflicts of interest.

For his own part, the Chief created a new Cabinet post and a new government agency to oversee it all. Soon he was ready to present someone to the Assembly, who was approved with great swiftness and enthusiasm because many of the Assembly

Members has lost their money to the Banksters' thievery.

The trial got underway and was broadcast live.

No Observers were allowed in the High Court, but a special room for them was provided so that they could monitor and report on every word, tone, facial expression and tic of the lawyers and the defendants.

The trial lasted for a month, which allowed the people of Oblivion to hear every detail of the betrayal perpetrated by the defendants. All of their usual distractions were forgotten while the trial was going on, because this affected the people directly, and they felt it intensely.

The verdicts came back after a day.

Guilty.

Guilty on all counts, all charges, all defendants.

The Book of Thieves

With that, the High Court moved on to the sentencing phase.

The people had mixed feelings about what they wanted.

Some people wanted the Thieves hung in public, others suggested time in a pillory, and still others suggested drawing and quartering. These ideas were straight out of old fairy tales.

But cruel and unusual punishments were illegal in the land of Oblivion, and that provision in the legal system was generally taken to mean physical punishments that were designed to mutilate, humiliate, and slowly kill.

Not to worry, the High Court Judges said, when told of these wishes.

There was another sort of punishment that was allowed, one that was very cruel but not unusual. After all, the law said not cruel AND unusual. It didn't say anything about punishments that were merely cruel.

The Book of Thieves

The Banksters and Dealers would have to surrender every last bit of wealth that they possessed – property, money, security, necessity, etc. – to the national treasury. They would have to give back the money to the people.

That wasn't all.

The groups that the Banksters had run were also to be taken away from them. The money that they had stashed in these groups was to become government property as well, along with the houses lost by the Dealers in the scams of their bosses.

The new agency that the Chief had established would be going over every house deed and having agents meet with every citizen who had lost a home in this scam, even if that meant searching the streets for the ones who were now homeless.

Anyone who could be given their house back would get it, with the benefit of the doubt weighted heavily on the side of the citizens rather than on the banks.

The Book of Thieves

That wasn't the only punishment in store for them.

The Thieves were all going to be put through a reeducation program so that they would understand that they were not special, not above the law, and not entitled to any of the things that they had stolen.

That still wasn't all.

The Banksters, Dealers, Key Holder, and Trustee were all going to spend the remainder of their natural lives in prison eating awful-tasting, cheap food. They would never be allowed to work in their chosen professions again.

The Thieves felt that this was a very cruel punishment indeed.

It was far worse than death…especially since the Thieves had no idea how long they would live. They would have to spend a lot of time alone, with nothing in their cells that would make suicide possible, constantly watched, and with no choice ever again about what they ate, what they wore, when they did anything, or who they saw.

They had no more control over their lives, which was fair because they had stolen that from so many others. Now they would feel that same misery with no end in sight.

About the Author

Stephanie C. Fox, J.D. is a historian, author, and editor. She is a graduate of William Smith College and the University of Connecticut School of Law, and she lives in Connecticut.

She runs *QueenBeeEdit*, an editing and publishing service, which caters to politicians, scientists, and others. See www.queenbeeedit.com for more of her work. Her imprint is *QueenBeeBooks*.

Ms. Fox has written several books on a variety of topics, including the effects of human overpopulation on the environment, Asperger's, cats, and travel to Kuwait and Hawai'i.

www.ingramcontent.com/pod-product-compliance
Lightning Source LLC
Chambersburg PA
CBHW050744030426
42336CB00012B/1646